LANDSICK

Genevieve Carver is a landlocked writer interested in connectivity and discord between human and non-human worlds. Her poetry has been published in journals including *Mslexia, The White Review, The North, The London Magazine, Magma* and *Poetry News*, and she won The Moth Nature Writing Prize in 2022, judged by Max Porter. Her first collection, *A Beautiful Way to be Crazy* (Verve Poetry Press), was based on her gig theatre show with a live band celebrating female experiences in the music industry; *Landsick* is her second poetry publication.

Also by Genevieve Carver

A Beautiful Way to be Crazy   (Verve Poetry Press, 2020)

Contents

Embrace	7
A Week Spent Leaving You	8
Stung	9
Grunions	10
Nature Documentary	11
Octopus	13
Confidences	14
Imploring the Hermit Crab to Embrace Her True Self	16
Cayton Bay	17
Whitby Goth Weekend	18
Low Tide	20
Ravenglass for Eskdale	21
David and the Whale	23
Landsick	24
Dream Thief	25
Interoception	26
Blue Monday	27
The Train and the Whale	28
Colour Chart	30
Urchin	31
Conch	32
Neanderthal in New York	34
Disappearing Islands	35
The Selkie Searches for Her Skin	36
High Tide	38
Playa Zicatela	39
Acknowledgements	41

ISBN: 978-1-915760-00-5

Cover designed by Aaron Kent

Edited & Typeset by Aaron Kent

Broken Sleep Books Ltd
Rhydwen
Talgarreg
Ceredigion
SA44 4HB

Broken Sleep Books Ltd
Fair View
St Georges Road
Cornwall
PL26 7YH

Landsick

Genevieve Carver

Embrace

We are langoustines feeling
for love on the ocean floor;
the hairs on our fingers that we
didn't even know were there
are tendrils reaching for something
solid in the dark, each drawing the other into
an embrace so close our bones begin to fuse,
blood flows freely between our veins

until, even as we sync sighs,
something catches in our breath.
Fibres harden, become our own again
and your mouth tastes suddenly of salt
as if the sea has flooded in between us,
forcing out my tongue.

A Week Spent Leaving You

You read a lot of books. Or perhaps
it's just the one book, but you read it a lot.
I go running, leave my high horse in the garage
drinking salt water. The coastline is being sick
all over itself. There are hairpin bends
all across the bed. The weather happens all at once.
Don't you know it's mathematically impossible
to photograph a rainbow. Physically then.
Just like you can't photograph someone's face
while they are sleeping, or they die. I try
with yours but you just keep on waking
up and living and now I'll never remember
the curve between your eyelids and your nose.
The TV is being sick all over itself.
All those bright colours. In Spanish, too.
Foreigners bombing the shit out of each other.
I make bets with myself. If Clinton wins the primaries
then I'll leave you. I make bets with your life
but you just keep on reading. We stand on
the cliff and watch the rocks take a battering.
You look me up and down as if you're
trying to photograph the slant of my neck
but you can't. Your eyes are sea glass beads.
We will always remember the angle of the rocks
reaching for the foam, despite the battering.
Let's have a cup of tea and talk about our future.
I make the tea with salt water. Our conversation
is sick all over itself. We can't leave Spain like this,
skid marks all across the finish line.
Someone will have to clean up.

Stung

The rock pools shone like lanterns
the bodies on the beach   fragmented
the barking of a dog became an impatient knock
on the door of your bedroom last summer
all the grains of sand were different sizes
the Frisbee or the dog was the wrong size
the castle on the cliff fell down and rebuilt itself all wrong
the old dead king inside woke up and declared war on Bridlington
we spoke openly   *because I might die*   we laughed
I dreamed of crowded streets and shouting
I said *I'm sorry I haven't had the time*
I dreamed of soft brown tentacles
I wondered if things   we   I
might be different after the swelling subsided.

Grunions

beach themselves
in order to mate
only loving for as long as they can   hold
their breath

wait for spring tide
make a dash for it by moonlight
fins become feet   or wings
on the sand

don't hide from the pelican's bill
but dance in plain sight
hoping to ward off danger
by shining brightly together.

Nature Documentary

You know the one. Attenborough
in his prime. Swarthy. Trustworthy.
The orcas grinning like villains,
seal pup for a football

                    and *thwack* -

                                        suddenly you're
                                        nothing but rage.
                                        David! You shout.
                                        Do something, please!
                            but the tail-slapping is merciless

and before you've caught your breath
you're clamped in the jaws of joy
laughter shaking the teeth
from your head.

                                I can't keep up, says David,
                                wiping the tears from your face
                                only now he's your ex-boyfriend
                                                    twenty years on
                                        leaving you all over again.

The orcas are bigger
than you'd realised
and are responding badly to reason
but you just knuckle down
to the business of counting –

ten things I'm grateful for;
three things in the room
I've not noticed before – the orcas,
the sea, the film crew –

and now it's just a case of

inhaling   exhaling
in   and out
in   and out.

Octopus

It was all for love;
that's what made her take the empty wine bottle
to its toughened muscle with the raw
intent of a wronged wife from a 1970s thriller.
Four hearts not being tender enough,
she pummelled the slippery wretch
until it yielded love from its dead glands.
In Greece, they get them to start secreting love
by bashing their brains against a rock
but the stainless draining board was her altar.
She served it with a smile
and a *Chablis Blanc* from the reduced aisle
but somehow could not prevent her stomach
from trying to leap from her mouth.

Confidences

When I was eleven my mother
bought me a set of worry dolls;
six little listeners in pink and green yarn
from a market stall in town.
I told them about the names I was called at school
about my irrational fear of the dark
about why I wasn't actually so sure it was irrational
about dying – yes, even then it was a concern –
later on I told them about my nose
being so embarrassingly the wrong shape
about how I was going to *Hell*
but before then I'd have to sit through *Purgatory*

and the five of them just took it in
– perhaps there were only ever five –
they didn't pass judgement so I told them
some more things like about the Yangtze River dolphin
the man on our street who shouted *fucking Thatcher!*
into the wheelie bins and wore Tesco carrier bags on his feet
axe-murderers and rare tropical diseases
how people didn't like me because they didn't
take the time to get to know me properly

and the four of them nodded their fuzzy
woollen heads sympathetically.
When I told them about the Global Climate Emergency
they didn't even seem surprised
when another schoolgirl was shot dead in her pigtails
they said *we know, we know, we know*

and they gazed up at me like the three Magi
in a knitted nativity gazing up at the sky.

We shared a bottle of Jim Beam
and I began to talk about losing bits of myself;
sending vital parts off in packets addressed
to publishing houses and forgetting to include an S.A.E.
about waking in the night to check if I could still use a pen
in case I found I'd been extinguished
like a firefly softly stifled beneath the surface of a lake
about advertisements for makeup and breakfast cereal
that are meant to make you worry about the lines in your face
and the overspill of your gut when really you should be worrying
about something useful like the housing crisis

and they both looked tired.
One said, *I'm sorry, I can't take this anymore*
and shuffled off right out the living room door

and the other one just stared at me and shrugged.

Imploring the Hermit Crab to Embrace Her True Self

Come OUT of that closet you know was never yours, aren't you tired of pretending? Aren't you tired of the ill-fitting husk, the grit under your cuticles? I can hear your swan-winged soul rattling at the exoskeletal bars, see the true blueness bubbling in your blood. I can help you shine. Your jelly legs are dying to catwalk the strand. You want to walk forwards. You want to upstage the dancing millions who wave their red claws like a robotic murmuration, don't they know the collective is dead? I know because I saw it in an Adam Curtis documentary. You want to show off your lacey pincering secrets, blowing kisses to the scallops crying *Tonight Matthew, I will be ME!* You can do this. I know because eleven people Googled me last month. Let them look. The paparazzi gulls, the seedy squids with suckers down their knickers. The enlarged claw is for selfies, the tender flesh is for gorging let them   feast   their   eyes.

Cayton Bay

I'd argued with myself the whole way there
not joining in with the B-Movie script you all rehearsed
across me   the hot car constricting my innards
I climbed out of the rear window
strapped myself to the roof with the surfboards
the 1960s pastiche we couldn't shake off
I stared up at the conflicted sky and waited for rain
to wash me onto the moss-tufted cliff
shrug me from its chalk-bald scalp and into
silk-grey tears as far as the eye can shed
feeling no more real than the bloodshot limestone wreck
squinting out over the gambling sugar-scoffing town
the wellied walkers with their creatures   pointless
pointlessly I stared up at the conflicted sky and waited
for waves to rip the sickness from the pit of me
the melodrama I couldn't shake off
silk-grey tears as far as the eye can shed
I'd argued with myself the whole way there
and lost.

Whitby Goth Weekend

She's daubing on eyeliner thick as the 1990s
hairtips licked with dusky pink
all buckles and DMs and PVC straps
she's climbing the steps to the ruined abbey
God is blaspheming His fucking cock off

she's corseted tight as the 1700s
all buckles and lace and petticoat folds
she's spoiled her skirts with whale oil
she's boiling the blubber in fat vats
she's flensing the flesh from the bone

she's gutted and skinned and raw as the 1940s
a spectre in the fish market
she's slapping her flanks on the ice banks
she's ogling the boggle-eyed punters
as her blood pools on the flags

she's swindling the arcade sharks
she's scarred as Dracula's fang marks
all crinoline hoops and bodice and sleeves
embalmed with candy floss and chip shop grease
she's hourglass-curved as the 1890s

Zoltar's fortune machine is warning her
not to let opportunity knock in vain
opportunity is knocking on her veins
hopeful and rosy and bogus as the 1990s
Zoltar is spitting out tickets like a sickness

she's listing her victims by lamplight
she's lifting the mist with her wingtips
she's harpoon-sharp as the 1700s
under the whale bone arch
the ghost of a bowhead's mouth
wishing he would gulp her down
in a gallon of brine
so she could slip out to sea
through a hairline crack
in the baleen sheet
dissolve
herself
in
salt.

Low Tide

If you're quick you can get to the hermitage and back before the ocean notices there's a rope you can use and the rocks won't mind you stepping on them if you're quick and all things considered it's a better use of your time than building a castle in the sand which you only do so you can later watch it fall it's risky because you might get stuck there with God and although you've nothing against God He's (you feel like it is *He*) probably not at the top of your imaginary dinner party guest list which you have spent a good deal of time deliberating on and includes people with a bit more spark like Bjork though you probably think Bjork is unlikely to be hanging out at an abandoned hermitage and yes managing expectations is important but sometimes you just have to go and see   even now   especially now   when the granite is gasping for breath and thin white fingers close around the neck   now   before the surge returns before the lump builds in your throat only to splutter out bile and brine onto the shore asking the pale moon for one good reason why.

Ravenglass for Eskdale

Alight here for memories of grandparents,
mudflats, and sweat under Gore-Tex.

Strap on your walking boots, wrap up
the flapjacks in two layers of cling film

take your laminated Ordinance Survey map
follow the hachures until you reach the sky.

Go down to the beach, dip a toe
then yield squealing to the ocean

let it wash you out and up again
from Corkickle to Seascale.

Forget the bullies at school,
they've been drowned in Selker Bay.

Get lost in Skalderskew woods and emerge
in Younghusband. Die among the leaves

and let your flesh become mulch.
Your funeral will be at St Bees

and the cathedral chasm will hum with bees
or monks or friends who will miss you.

Passengers from Manchester may wish
to hold on extra tight, there are colours here

you've never seen. Slow down,
or you'll smudge the ink of the hills.

Take care to leave your personal belongings
on the train; you won't need them anymore.

David and the Whale

At 8:30 am on Friday 20 January 2006, David Dopin was on a train when he phoned the authorities to say that he believed he had been hallucinating, as he thought he had just spotted a whale swimming in the River Thames.

— *Wikipedia.*

David

My coffee was bitter and too hot / I spilt a dirty river on my leg / the pain opened a door / in swam the visions / what can you do but call the authorities / my mother didn't pick up / the pewter beak / the phalanxes of teeth / I held a bowling ball head in my hands and kissed a pillow of salt / before I shut my laptop I deleted all the files / the mud pressed up against the rattling windows / I surrendered myself to the flood.

The Whale

The monster was all tail / exoskeleton solid as turtle shell / two bright eyes like the will-o'-the-wisp of an angler fish / this wasn't in the guidebook / now I'm strapped in by the bridges / I don't believe in Dopin for a second / cited nowhere but Wikipedia and far too close to *dolphin* / here come the shakes / I can't hear myself think but I know what I've seen.

The Train

It's been three days and I've yet to leave the depot / the doctor signed me off / the nausea / the dizzy spells / the concrete wall brings solace / but there's water on the tracks / everything is slipping / a liquid chaos you can't contain in a paper cup / the infestation I ingest each morning / the world beyond Slade Green is trembling.

Landsick

The tug of the magician's tablecloth
leaves you quivering, not shattered

the bucking of your five year plan
demands limbs to splay in ways

twelve weeks of yoga could
never have prepared you for

your birthday is leaning from an upper
storey window, threatening to jump

the reservoir is unmoved by the rings you run
the bargains you attempt make with time

about the bathroom renovation, says the land,
about those promises whispered through wine

and, somewhere far away, *sshh now,*
sssssssshhhhhhhhh, says the sea.

Dream Thief

You tell me you dreamed of *a shipwreck,*
a blue wind and long, white sands
I don't know if you're trying to impress me
but we both know that dream should have been mine –
it's got my signature whiff of reheated leftovers /
crab shack melancholia all over it,
the landscape-as-passive-aggressor motif,
the hallmark smirk in the clinkered hull.

But then you were always like that, *yes*, you were.
Even in the early days, seeing out the dusk
on the narrow boat deck, your fingers coping
with the stem of a wine glass, drinking in
my summer haze, *my* water boatmen,
my anaemic moon rising, snatching away *my* punchline
as the sun drained from the lock,
tucking it into the ripples in the faces of *my* friends.

I keep finding you in my poems, moving
punctuation around & corecting my spelling.
Always trying to get inside me.
Even my dreams.
OK, you added some of your own
detail and I guess it wasn't bad.
I never would have thought of those fossilised trees
sticking up from the beach like the ghosts of lampposts

and I never would have got us out alive –
I'd have sat on my haunches until dawn
picking at the salt-bleached bones of you.

Interoception

We love each other don't we, so it doesn't matter who gave who the worms, we said. But it did matter, it mattered because I could feel them moving up and down like commuter trains, and not just in the gut, either. There are some things you feel from the inside out, like government bulletins. Writing themselves on your bowels until you're nothing but entrails. So we swallowed our pills and waited for the little bastards to die, but they only did in body. The creases in the brain where it tastes of lemon curd and four-year-old you is vomiting up her dinner because she overdid it again. Who cares what they're saying on Twitter, my pain receptors have been replaced by silk. Who cares if the living parts of me are not my own. I'd rather rot.

Blue Monday

You leave for work without your wallet.
I stay home in my dressing gown, Googling
how to apologise when you've hurt someone you love,
how to be productive when you're sad.
One site recommends standing regularly,
crying *privately*, taking frequent breaks;
another suggests *adding a splash of blue to your workspace.*
I put on my bluest jumper but it's grey
and now I'm fifty shades of whale
stranded and gasping in the buttermilk room.
I buy a tin of *Cornflower Dream* and coat the walls.
I write words like *cobalt / azure / sorry* on cigarette papers
scrunch them up, swallow them like Class A's
wash them down with Bombay Sapphire.
I listen to blue music like *Rhapsody in Blue, Blue Monday*
and *Blue Moon*, but not blues music because it's too blue.
You come home, demanding to know what's going on,
where the hot taps have gone. My apology isn't ready.
I'm drowning, I say, stitching you into the hem of my jeans
and dragging you under, sinking us right down
through the floorboards, all the way
to the bottom of the deep blue sea.

The Train and the Whale

In November 2020 a metro train that overran the stop blocks at a station outside Rotterdam was saved from plummeting 10m into the water below by a giant plastic sculpture of a whale's tail.

THE TRAIN: It's not what it looks like.

THE WHALE: Nor am I.

THE TRAIN: I'm stranded.

THE WHALE: You've suffered an uncoupling.

THE TRAIN: The yellow jackets are taking measurements.

THE WHALE: You should have been listening.

THE TRAIN: I couldn't hear over the shrill blue noise of whalesong.

THE WHALE: You should have been watching for the signs.

THE TRAIN: They've taken a swab from the signal points.

THE WHALE: Did you notice the black-backed gulls overhead?

THE TRAIN: Splash me in oil and put me on a stretcher of steel.

THE WHALE: The ones now pecking out your eyes.

THE TRAIN: Release me into the diesel sea where I can swim free.

THE WHALE: You should spend a bit of time on *you*.

THE TRAIN: Under the water are you smirking through your baleen?

THE WHALE: Have a bubble bath. Put a favourite record on.

THE TRAIN: When are you coming up for air?

THE WHALE: For the nightmares, try a sleep app.

THE TRAIN: How much longer can you hold me?

Colour Chart

the peeled pink of shrimp boiled alive in its skin

the seared pink of scallop

the squeaking pink of newborn mice

the raw pink of mince weeping watercolour blood

the pink that's purple left out in the rain

the pink that's red with its pants pulled down

the blushing pink of Barbie's car

the broken pinkie promises

the cute pink of ribbons in platinum plaits

the pink that's hot   baby   princess

cherry blossom   Himalayan salt

      flamingo   bubble gum   lip gloss   dawn

         peony   rose petal   axolotl   quartz

as a child I always hated pink

      later
         I learned to hate myself

the pink parts of me

Urchin

The morning after
you shouldn't have felt obliged
to excavate the brittle spine
from my frayed flesh

it was pure kindness
the way you kept on asking
if I was alright
if it hurt

as I pushed the words
I'm fine   don't stop
out from behind
a glistening screen.

Conch

the irony is you're   earless

eyestalks edge from their notches
the seabed is
                                    silence

the swish of sand is   silent
leap of muscular foot

the schlepp of your ending is

                                soundless

rubbery flesh shucked
down a loggerhead's gullet

the human hands are   wordless

that pluck you from the shingle
daub ochre in your open cleft
insert a mouthpiece
to your corkscrew tip
lift you to lips and
make   you   sing

          sing yourself to sleep
for 18,000 years on the cave floor
80 more in a French museum
until new breath wakes you

the three   notes
                    ringing   out

at 100 decibels
as loud as a power drill
a snowmobile
a human baby crying
iPhone headphones turned up to the max

Neanderthal in New York

The cave entrances are fireless / the darkest parts are artless / there's little to hunt but fat black rats / I scavenged a carcass from the oblate floor / boneless and sea-tasting / let me tell you something about caves / the magic is song-spun but you've forgotten the tune / strip-lit noise / I caught a show in Broadway and I couldn't see the sky / I gave it three stars / I went to Ground Zero and glued my ear to the earth / respects are something you pay but you can pay in other ways / I walked through Central Park and somebody shouted *flat-chested bitch!* / when I learn about war I will assume this to be one / the donut I liked at first – that cloudberry tang – but all too quickly sick-making, far too much.

Disappearing Islands

Santorini caldera

It is said the land's knuckles
surface and sink like crocodiles
sliding under mangrove silk
with barely a nostril twitch
even a fisherman's careful eye
can never be sure he isn't missing
a sharp dark spike in the wine-dark skyline
already dawn's rosy fingers are blistering
so pupils are adjusted to the cool white shade
maps are consulted – but somebody swears
the yellowing paper has been altered
the gods pretend to laugh
as they shake out their towels
but Zeus's smile suggests he too is uncertain
and there's a slight discolouration
in the photograph on your mantelpiece
a fragment snagging your thought train
a last ripple shivered through the dim bright din.

The Selkie Searches for Her Skin

I combed the nooks of Ravenscar
where seals haul out on rocks
like turkey breasts on stainless worktops
but all I found was the discarded nylon raincoat
of a drowned or disillusioned tourist –
needless to say it didn't fit.
At Robin Hood's Bay I crawled into an outlaw's cave
where I stubbed my toe on a treasure chest,
oak-thick and gilded and the size of a swollen fist.
I locked myself inside and lay perfectly still
counting the seconds between the waves
until the tide came in. I floated away on a six foot
swell and washed up in my lover's bed.
I peeled off his sheets and disembowelled the pillows
until feathers flew about the room like a goose
being shot or a scene from a bad romcom.
I opened up drawers full of socks and letters
from the council. I even opened the letters and wrote
replies saying *Please, Chamber of Local Representatives,
have you seen my skin?* I needed bottles
to put the letters in so I drank my lover's gin.
I pushed back all the bookcases to look for
secret doors. I broke down the doors and raided
the faerie kingdoms until the Little People wept.
The last time I had it I was eleven. No twelve.
I don't remember seals but I remember eggs
being cracked irrevocably into a frying pan,
the way this made me cry. My lover came home
and cradled my pain in his ego. *Where had I been
all this time?* He'd have to phone the coastguard,
call the search party off. I tried to fob him off

with my #2minutebeachclean bit
but the plastic sack in my hand was empty
as a pelt strewn on the taxidermist's floor.

High Tide

My cove is full of love again;
it's in the pockets of the bladderwrack,
the tiny hearts of winkle and whelk.
The gutweed is tied up in knots of love
the open mouths of anemones
are breathing love in and out
the gobies and blennies are washing
their beeswing fins in love
the hermit crab has moved in with love
and taken out a mortgage
the mermaid's purse is overspilling with love
the sailors are cashing fat cheques of love
the spaniels are splashing their paws in love
and the walkers are lovers holding hands

but the moon draws love from far away
from a distant bay where prickly cockle
husks pepper the shingle strand
and redshanks raid the lugworms
struggling in the sand
where gulls bicker over
vinegar-soaked fake news
and a shipwrecked dolphin heaves
its last exhausted gasp
where the devil crab scuttles
from its hiding place
and you hole up below the surface;
a weever fish waiting
for love to return.

Playa Zicatela

Everything is balls-out;
the cocksure dogs who own the dust of the streets
the men arranged on towels like Greek statues in museums –
flesh bronzed, oiled and tattooed with floral skulls, *vive sin miedo*
the stingrays who leap clean out of the water
the fisherman who tells me
that *only the males do that*
the pelicans who swallow the lot in one clean gulp
the ocean that swaggers onto shore
the sun that spanks the concrete from the roofs.

I think of all those English men
the ones who hid behind me
in bedrooms with posters of Kurt Cobain on the wall
quoted Kerouac to assure me of the men they weren't
the ones skulking in the back rooms of pubs
fingers gripped around cold pints and pool cues
and our sun afraid to show its face
and the opaque sky   crying suddenly in public
but never explaining why   and our version of the sea
not quite knowing how to touch the land.

Acknowledgements

Thank you to the editors of the following publications, where many of these poems first appeared: *The White Review, The North, Mslexia, The London Magazine, Obsessed with Pipework, Northern Gravy, Under The Radar, Envoi, Poetry News, Tears in the Fence, osmosispress. com* and *Waymaking: an anthology of women's adventure writing, poetry and art* (Vertebrae Publishing 2018).

This small book has been a long time in the making, and enormous thanks are due to its early readers: Ben Dorey, Suzannah Evans and Oliver Mantell. A special thank you to Isabel Galleymore for mentoring me through later stages and submission – you helped me to become bolder, freer and more myself as a writer.

Thanks are also due to Aaron Kent and the whole team at Broken Sleep Books for believing in my work and giving it a home.

Many of these poems were born between clifftop, beach, rockpool and wave, especially along the raw bright shores of the Yorkshire coast. The North Sea washes into the words I write and is the antidote when the land makes me sick.

Thank you to my ever-supportive friends and family, and especially to Chris for being the keel that steadies, no matter how rough the storm.

LAY OUT YOUR UNREST

Milton Keynes UK
Ingram Content Group UK Ltd.
UKHW041846101023
430330UK00004B/180

BANDAGED DREAMS

Emma Filtness (she/her) is a poet and Senior Lecturer in Creative Writing at Brunel University London. She particularly enjoys exploring found and visual poetics. Twitter: @em_filtness

Also by Emma Filtness

The Venus Atmosphere   (Steel Incisors, 2022)